The People of Russia and Their Food

by Ann L. Burckhardt

C A P S T O N E   P R E S S

MANKATO, MINNESOTA

C A P S T O N E   P R E S S

818 North Willow Street • Mankato, Minnesota 56001

Printed in the United States of America.

Library of Congress Cataloging-in-Publication Data
Burckhardt, Ann, 1933-
    The people of Russia and their food / by Ann L. Burckhardt
    p. cm. -- (Multicultural cookbooks)
  Includes bibliographical references and index.
  Summary: Describes food customs and preparation in Russia, regional dishes, and cooking techniques; includes recipes for a variety of meals.
    ISBN 1-56065-432-5
  1. Cookery, Russian--Juvenile literature. 2. Food habits--Russia (Federation) --Juvenile literature. 3. Russia (Federation)--Social life and customs--Juvenile literature. [1. Cookery, Russian. 2. Food habits--Russia (Federation). 3. Russia (Federation)--Social life and customs.] I. Title. II. Series.
    TX723.3.B87   1996
    394.1'0947--dc20   96-24787
                                      CIP
                                      AC

Photo credits
Jean S. Buldain, cover, 14, 23, 28.
Stokka Productions, cover inset, 18, 26, 32, 36, 42.
FPG, 4, 6, 16, 25, 40.
International Stock, 10, 12.

Lisa Fechter, food stylist
Carla Chesley, chef
Cover dish: Cabbage stir-fry
Props: Pier 1 Imports

Table of Contents

Fast Facts about Russia

Location: Northern Asia and eastern Europe

Size: 6.6 million square miles (17 million square kilometers)

Population: 149.6 million

Capital: Moscow

Language: Russian

Religion: Russian Orthodox plus Muslim, Roman Catholic, Baptist, Lutheran, Evangelist, and Jewish.

Climate: Long, cold winters and short, hot summers

Money: Ruble

Siberia is heavily forested. It has many birch trees.

Chapter 1
The Country

Russia is huge. It is the largest country in the world. It covers major parts of the continents of Europe and Asia. Russia is twice as large as Canada, which is the second largest country.

The Ural Mountains divide the European part of Russia and the Asian part. The European part is to the west. Most of the European section is a flat plain. Big cities with industries are there. The Asian section is to the east. Siberia is in the Asian part. Not many people live there. It has harsh, long winters.

For many years, Russia was the leading nation in the Union of Soviet Socialist Republics.

People walk to work at the Kremlin in Moscow.

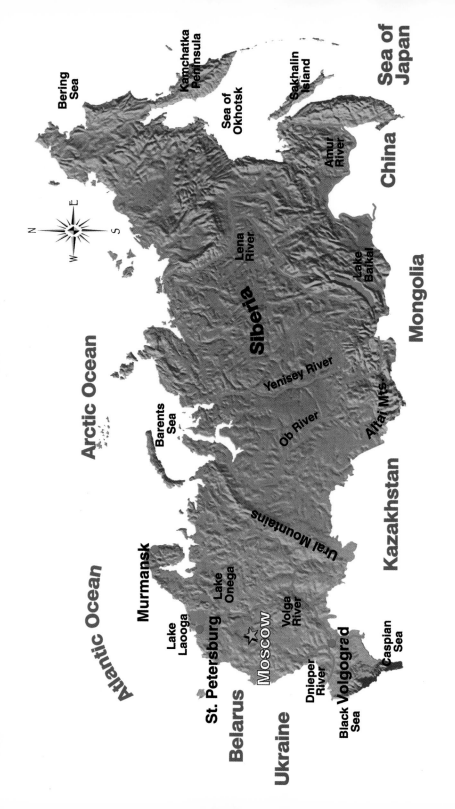

Bering Sea

Kamchatka Peninsula

Sea of Okhotsk

Sakhalin Island

Sea of Japan

Amur River

China

Lena River

Lake Baikal

Siberia

Mongolia

Yenisey River

Arctic Ocean

Barents Sea

Ob River

Altai Mts

Kazakhstan

Ural Mountains

Atlantic Ocean

Murmansk

Lake Onega

Lake Laooga

St. Petersburg

Moscow

Volga River

Belarus

Dnieper River

Caspian Sea

Volgograd

Ukraine

Black Sea

N E S W

But in 1991, the Soviet Union broke apart. Russia became the main country in the new Commonwealth of Independent States. Russia is now a democracy.

Russia has rich natural resources. These include forests, farmland, minerals, and streams to harness for electric power. The best farms are in a region called the Black Earth Belt.

About 150 million people live in Russia. Three-fourths of the Russian people live in cities. Others live in villages near farms. Many of the people are poor. Moscow is the capital of Russia. It has 8 million people. St. Petersburg has more than 4 million people.

Many Russians love to read books and newspapers. They read to keep up with world affairs. During its long history, Russia has produced many famous authors, playwrights, and composers.

Ballet is a favorite entertainment. The Bolshoi Ballet in Moscow is known around the world.

Russia also has many museums. People enjoy going to museums to see artworks and exhibits.

Chapter 2

The Market

Shopping for food is an almost daily activity in Russia. Many people live in small apartments. Storage space is limited and it is best to buy often. Every morning, a family member goes out to buy food for the day.

Two or three generations of a family may share an apartment. They also share the shopping. Sometimes the shoppers will go to a big grocery store. But usually they will go to a nearby farmers' market. There they buy food from the family who grew it. In some places, produce is flown in by airplane from the farm to the market.

Food from the republics of Georgia and Azerbaijan is sold at the central market in Moscow.

Russian farmers sell potatoes.

These outdoor farmers' markets are colorful. They have rows of tables covered with produce. In the late summer and early fall, there are apples, pears, carrots, beets, eggplants, beans, and tomatoes. Flowers, honey, cheeses, spices, eggs, handmade crafts, and clothing might be for sale, too.

Most Russian women have jobs outside the home. They sometimes have to shop on their way home from work. Shoppers may have to wait in line to buy things like bread and meat. Because of the many shortages in the past, Russians are used to lining up to get what they need.

Fortunately, Russian cooks are good at figuring out how to use what is available. Cabbage, carrots, potatoes, apples, and sour cream are foods that are used often. They are used in a wide variety of recipes.

Russians who live in large cities usually travel by train or subway. That is another reason to buy things in smaller quantities. They buy just what they can carry in a woven shopping bag.

Mushrooms are a favorite wild food in Russia. In the spring and fall, people take a holiday to go mushroom picking in the countryside. The strong, earthy smell of the mushrooms fills the train when they ride home.

Chapter 3

A Celebration

The churches in Russia are colorful and beautifully decorated. They are topped with onion-shaped domes. No two domes are alike. The dome-covered churches are the churches of the Russian Orthodox religion.

Easter is the biggest event of the Russian Orthodox church year. Christians believe Jesus Christ rose from the dead on that day. Russians go to church at midnight on the Saturday before Easter. More services are held Easter Sunday.

Easter eggs are carefully decorated with very detailed patterns. First the whites and yolks are blown out of the egg shells. Then the shells are covered with a design and painted. The eggs are

St. Basil's Cathedral in Moscow attracts many visitors.

works of art. The decorating method is passed from parent to child.

The eggs are taken to the church to be blessed. They are displayed, admired, and kept for the next Easter.

Easter dinner is festive. It has many courses. People are happy that Lent, a period of fasting, is over and the cold winter will soon end.

A special food is served at Easter. It is an Easter bread called kulich. You will find the recipe for kulich on page 38. It is baked to look like a dome of a Russian church.

Onion-shaped domes top Russian Orthodox churches.

Chapter 4
Main Dishes

Russians eat cabbage nearly every day. It is served in many ways. It is used as a filling in turnovers and as the main ingredient in soups and salads. Cabbage is good source of vitamin C.

Turnovers are popular in Russia and all over Eastern Europe. They are filled with vegetables, cottage cheese, chopped meat, fried onions, or even fruit. Sometimes the covering is flaky like a pie crust. Turnovers are a nice way to use leftovers.

Russian farmers raise cattle, pigs, sheep, and chickens. The Russian people use the meat in many ways.

Cabbage stir-fry

Cabbage-filled Turnovers

1 teaspoon vegetable oil
2/3 cup onion, chopped
2 cups shredded cabbage or packaged coleslaw mix
1 tablespoon brown sugar
1 teaspoon lemon juice
1 teaspoon dill weed
dash of salt and pepper
7-1/2-ounce can refrigerated buttermilk biscuits

To make filling, pour vegetable oil in large skillet. Add onion and coleslaw mix. Stir to coat vegetables with oil. Add brown sugar, lemon juice, dill weed, salt, and pepper. Cook and stir until vegetables are tender, about 8 minutes. Remove from heat and cool.

To make crust, you will need a rolling pin, two squares of waxed paper, and a baking sheet. Preheat oven to 400 degrees. Open the biscuits. One at a time, place a biscuit between the pieces of waxed paper. Roll it out until it is about 4 inches across. Remove waxed paper.

Place a heaping tablespoon of cabbage mixture in the center of each biscuit. Fold biscuit over, closing in the filling. Seal the edges together with a fork. Arrange turnovers on baking sheet. Bake 8 to 10 minutes, or until golden brown. Serve right away or let cool to room temperature. Makes 10 turnovers.

Cabbage Stir-fry

1 onion, chopped
2 tablespoons vegetable oil
2 cups packaged coleslaw mix
5 hot dogs, cut into 1/2-inch slices
salt and pepper

Heat the oil in a 12-inch skillet. When oil is hot, add the coleslaw mix. Cook and stir over medium-high heat 3 to 5 minutes. Add hot dog slices. Season to taste with salt and pepper.

Cook and stir 5 more minutes until heated through. Serves 4.

Fruit-sweetened Beef

8 ounces tender beef like sirloin
2 teaspoons oil
2/3 cup prunes
salt to taste

Cut the beef into small pieces. Heat the oil in a small skillet. Start frying the beef pieces in the oil. Add the prunes. Cover the skillet and cook over medium-low heat until the prunes have plumped up. They will soak up some of the meat juices.

Add salt to taste. Serve hot. Serves 4.

Kitchen smarts: This goes well with mashed potatoes or fried potatoes.

A farmer near St. Petersburg stands with his dairy cattle.

Chicken Baked in Sour Cream

2-1/2 to 3 pound broiler-fryer chicken
2/3 cup sour cream

Preheat oven to 375 degrees. Wash the chicken and pat dry with paper towels. Rub the inside of the chicken with salt. Place the chicken with its breast up in a shallow roasting pan. If you have a roasting rack, put that under the bird.

Spread sour cream on the chicken. Bake the chicken for 1-1/2 hours.

To tell whether the chicken is done, stick a fork into it and look at the juices that run out. If the juices run clear and not pink, the bird is done. Serves 4 to 6.

Shepherds tend their sheep in Siberia.

Chapter 5
Side Dishes

Buckwheat is a popular Russian grain. It grows well in cold climates. It is used to make the Russian favorite called kasha.

Kasha is a grain dish. It is also known as buckwheat groats. Kasha is often served plain with meats and stews. It is served instead of potatoes or rice.

Potatoes are also popular in Russia. Potato pancakes are easy to make and taste good.

The delicious thin pancakes are like French crepes. They can be eaten with your fingers or with a knife and fork.

Potato pancakes

Kasha

2 cups beef broth, chicken broth or water
2 tablespoons butter or margarine
1/2 teaspoon salt
dash pepper
1 egg or egg white
1 cup buckwheat groats

In a medium pan, heat broth, butter or margarine, salt, and pepper.

In a small bowl, beat egg or egg white. Stir in the buckwheat groats. Stir until the groats are coated with egg. Put the groats in a frying pan. Stir over medium-high heat 2 to 3 minutes. Stir until the egg is cooked and is no longer transparent. The groats should not be in clumps.

Bring broth or water to a boil. Quickly pour over groats. Cover the frying pan tightly with a lid. Cook over low heat 8 to 11 minutes. When it is done, the kasha kernels will be tender and the liquid will be soaked up. Serves 6.

A Russian woman rakes grass.

Easy Potato Pancakes

1-1/4 cups frozen hash-brown potatoes, thawed
1 egg
2 tablespoons milk
1 tablespoon flour
1/2 teaspoon salt
dash pepper
vegetable oil
sour cream

Measure then thaw hash browns. In a medium bowl, beat the egg and milk. Add potatoes, flour, salt, and pepper. Mix well.

Heat a griddle over medium heat. Pour in just enough vegetable oil to coat the surface.

Use a 1/4-cup measuring cup to drop potato mixture on the hot griddle. You can make more than one pancake at a time. Fry 3 minutes, or until bottom is browned and crisp. Turn and brown the other side. Serve immediately.

Top with sour cream. Makes 6 to 8 small pancakes.

Kitchen smarts: Applesauce is delicious served with potato pancakes.

Thin Pancakes

2/3 cup milk
2/3 cup water
2 eggs
pinch of salt
1 cup flour
vegetable oil
sour cream
minced pickled herring
jam

In a medium bowl, mix milk and water. Add eggs, salt, and flour. Beat well. Let the batter stand and thicken while heating a 7-inch skillet. Pour a little oil into the hot skillet. Immediately pour about 3 tablespoons of batter into the skillet. Lift the skillet, tilting it so that the batter coats the entire bottom. When the pancake is light brown on the bottom, carefully turn it over using a spatula. Cook until light brown on other side. Keep frying pancakes until batter is gone.

Stack pancakes on a plate with waxed paper between them. Cover with a towel to keep them from drying out. Spread them with sour cream, minced pickled herring, or jam. Roll them up or fold into quarters or triangles. Makes 10 to 12 pancakes.

Chapter 6

Soup and Salad

When they think of Russia, many people think of borscht. It is a red soup made from beets. Borscht uses all of the least expensive and most common ingredients found in Russia. There are probably as many recipes for borscht as there are kitchens in Russia.

Borscht is best made a day ahead. Then the flavors can blend. Serve hot with rye bread as the main course for a simple meal. Or borscht can be the first course of a festive dinner.

Russian salad is popular all over Europe, not just in Russia. Some of the vegetables in the salad are cooked. Other salad vegetables are pickled. Sometimes diced beets are added. This turns the salad a deep pink.

Apple-potato salad and borscht

Vegetable Borscht

16-ounce can whole beets, drained and grated
2 potatoes, peeled and cut into 1/2-inch cubes
1 quart water
1 tablespoon vegetable oil
1 onion, minced
1 carrot, peeled and grated
1 tomato, chopped
5 whole peppercorns
3 bay leaves
sour cream
snipped parsley or dill

Drain and grate the beets. This is very messy. Grate over a bowl in a sink or over newspapers. Be sure to wear an apron. Set the beets aside.

In a soup kettle, heat water to boiling. Add the potatoes. Cook until almost fork-tender.

In the meantime, heat oil in a skillet. Stir in the onion. Add carrot and continue cooking.

When the potatoes are almost fork-tender, add the beets, onion, carrot, and tomato. Stir in the peppercorns and bay leaves. Simmer 5 minutes, then remove from heat. Put on the lid until ready to eat. Serve with sour cream and snipped parsley or dill. Serves 6 to 8.

Apple-Potato Salad

1 pint potato salad
1/2 cucumber, peeled and chopped
1/2 cup frozen peas
1 small apple, cored and shredded
1 carrot, peeled and shredded
mayonnaise or yogurt, if needed

Put potato salad in a medium bowl. Put peas in a strainer. Hold under hot-water faucet until the ice is off the peas.

Add cucumber, peas, apple, and carrot to the potato salad. Mix well. Mayonnaise or yogurt may be added if needed to hold the salad together.

Add salt and pepper to taste. Cover the salad. Chill until time to serve. Serves 6.

Kitchen smarts: This salad is good with cooked diced chicken or tuna added.

Chapter 7
Bread and Dessert

Russians drink cup after cup of hot black tea. With it, they enjoy breads and desserts.

Frozen sweet-roll dough can be used to make easy versions of popular Russian bread and dessert.

The frozen dough is used to make the Easter bread called kulich. It is baked to look like a Russian Orthodox church tower with a dome on top.

The dough is also used to make a delicious poppy seed cake.

Poppy seed cake

Easter Sweet Bread

1 pound frozen sweet dough, thawed
shortening
flour
2 tablespoons raisins
1 tablespoon chopped almonds
3 empty 16-ounce food cans (3-1/2 inches high)
vanilla frosting

Wash and dry the cans. Grease inside of cans with shortening. Divide the dough into three equal parts. Spread a little flour on a work surface. Using your knuckles, punch the dough down to get rid of air bubbles. Top each dough piece with raisins and chopped almonds. Work them into the dough by folding the dough over and over. Shape the dough into a smooth ball about 3 inches across. Put into a prepared can. Repeat for other two cans.

Let dough rise in warm part of the kitchen until it is about even with the top of the can. This will take 35 to 40 minutes. Take top rack out of the oven. Move the other rack to the lowest level. Preheat oven to 350 degrees.

Bake the loaves in their cans 25 to 35 minutes. A domed top will form as the loaf rises. When loaf is medium brown, take the can out of the oven. Remove loaf. If sides are not golden, bake 5 minutes more. Cool briefly. Frost with vanilla frosting. Serves 12.

Poppy Seed Cake

1 pound sweet roll dough, thawed
flour
8-ounce can poppy seed filling
3/4 cup finely chopped walnuts

Preheat oven to 350 degrees. Sprinkle a little flour on a work surface. Use a rolling pin to roll dough as thin as you can. The flat work surface should be at a height where you can put some pressure on the rolling pin as you work.

Spread dough with poppy seed filling and sprinkle with walnuts. Roll up tightly beginning at a wide side. Seal well by pinching edges of roll together. Put the roll on a lightly greased baking sheet. Be sure to have the sealed edge underneath. Pull the ends around to form a crescent moon.

Bake 25 to 30 minutes, until golden brown. To serve, cut in 1-inch slices. Serve as a dessert or with tea any time. Serves 12 to 14.

Metric Measurements Chart

Use the chart below to convert recipe amounts in standard units to metric units.

Volume

1 teaspoon = 5 milliliters
1 tablespoon = 15 milliliters
1 fluid ounce = 30 milliliters
1 cup = 0.24 liter
1 pint = 0.47 liter
1 quart = 0.95 liter
(to convert liters to quarts, multiply by 1.06)

Weight

1 ounce = 28 grams
1 pound = 0.45 kilogram
2.2 pounds = 1 kilogram
(to convert grams to ounces, multiply by .035)

A vendor in Moscow sells pears.

Kitchen Safety

Here are some guidelines for cooking success.

1. Before cooking, read through the entire recipe. Make sure you understand each step. Clear your work space of odds and ends. Turn off the radio and television. Then you can concentrate.

2. Get out all the ingredients and equipment that you will need. Then, if something is missing, you can find a substitute.

3. Wash your hands completely before you start and as needed while cooking. Do not forget the backs of your hands and the spaces between your fingers. Always wash the fruits and vegetables you will be preparing, too.

4. You work best and safest when the work space is at the right height. You might need to stand on a stool for the best arm motion while cutting or stirring.

Get out all the equipment you need before starting to cook.

5. Sharp knives and peelers require respect. Ask someone older to give you a hand with cutting, chopping, and slicing. Remember to move the peeler away from yourself. Always use a clean cutting board.

6. Protect yourself from burns. Always use a hot pad or mitt with hot pans. Turn the handles of pots and pans to the back of the range. Then you will not bump into them. Keep baking soda or salt close by to sprinkle on the flames if something catches fire. Never put water on a grease fire.

7. Try to clean up as you cook. If you have to wait for something to boil or bake, use that time to wash bowls and pans. Then put things away. Those who share your kitchen will thank you.

Cooking Glossary

beat—to stir thoroughly until blended
boil—to heat a liquid over high heat until bubbles form and rise rapidly to the surface
grate—to cut food into tiny pieces using a special utensil
preheat—to allow an oven to reach the desired baking temperature before use
produce—fresh fruits and vegetables
shred—to tear or cut into small pieces
simmer—to heat something to just below boiling
spatula—utensil with long, blunt blade
stir-fry—to cook quickly at a high heat
thaw—to allow frozen food to reach room temperature

To Learn More

Lapenkova, Valentina and Edward Lambton. *Russian Food and Drink.* New York: The Bookwright Press, 1988.

Lerner Geography Department. *Russia.* Minneapolis: Lerner Publications, 1992.

Plotkin, Gregory and Sima Plotkin. *Cooking the Russian Way.* Minneapolis: Lerner Publications, 1986.

Schomp, Virginia. *Russia: New Freedoms, New Challenges.* New York: Marshall Cavendish, 1996.

Useful Addresses and Internet Sites

Russian-American Center
2670 Leavenworth
San Francisco, CA 94133
e-mail: trac@dna1.com

World Learning
P.O. Box 676
Brattleboro, VT 05302-0676

Friends and Partners: Welcome

http://solar.rtd.utk.edu/friends/home/htmlopt-tables-mac-english-

Russia on the Web

http://www.valley.net:80/~transnat/

Russian Page

http://www.vicnet.net.au/vicnet.country/russia/htm

Russlinks

http://users.aimnet.com/~ksyrah/ekskurs/russlink.html

Index

apple-potato salad, 35

baked chicken, 24
Bolshoi Ballet, 9
borscht, 33, 34
buckwheat, 27

cabbage stir-fry, 21

Easter, 15, 16
Easter sweet bread, 38

farmers' market, 11, 12
fruit-sweetened beef, 23

kasha, 27, 29
kulich, 17, 37

Moscow, 9

poppy seed cake, 37, 39
potato pancakes, 27, 30

Russian Orthodox, 15

St. Petersburg, 9

thin pancakes, 27, 31
turnovers, 19, 20

Ural Mountains, 7